AWESOME

Dinosaur Jokes

for Kids

Bob Phillips

HARVEST HOUSE™ PUBLISHERS

EUGENE, OREGON

Cover by Terry Dugan Design, Minneapolis, Minnesota

AWESOME DINOSAUR JOKES FOR KIDS
Copyright © 2002 by Bob Phillips
Published by Harvest House Publishers
Eugene, Oregon 97402

ISBN 0-7369-0752-1

Printed in the United States of America.

02 03 04 05 06 07 08 09 / BC-MS / 10 9 8 7 6 5 4 3 2 1

Contents

1

Dinosaur Mania

First dinosaur: Did you hear the joke about the rotten dinosaur eggs?
Second dinosaur: No.
First dinosaur: Two bad!

First dinosaur: Did you hear about the ten tons of woolly mammoth hair stolen from the wig-maker today?
Second dinosaur: No, I haven't.
First dinosaur: The police are now combing the area.

First dinosaur: How do you stop a dinosaur from biting his nails?
Second dinosaur: I give up.
First dinosaur: Pull his foot out of his mouth.

First dinosaur: Oxygen was discovered in 1773.
Second dinosaur: What did dinosaurs breathe
    before then?

First dinosaur: Which is farthest away, Australia
    or the sun?
Second dinosaur: Australia.
First dinosaur: What makes you think that?
Second dinosaur: I can see the sun from here.

First dinosaur: Ask me if I'm a rabbit.
Second dinosaur: Okay. Are you a rabbit?
First dinosaur: Yes, I'm a rabbit. Now ask me if
    I'm a dinosaur.
Second dinosaur: I'm game. Are you a dinosaur?
First dinosaur: No, you silly. I told you I'm a
    rabbit.

First dinosaur: Why did George Washington cut
    down a cherry tree?
Second dinosaur: Hmm. You got me stumped!

First dinosaur: I used to be a big-game hunter. Why, for years I shot woolly mammoths in Alaska.
Second dinosaur: That's impossible! There aren't any woolly mammoths in Alaska.
First dinosaur: Of course not. I shot them all.

First dinosaur: What kind of math do owls like?
Second dinosaur: Owl-gebra.

First dinosaur: What kind of bears like to go out in the rain?
Second dinosaur: Drizzly bears.

First dinosaur: What do snake charmers wear around their necks?
Second dinosaur: Boa-ties.

First dinosaur: What do snakes learn in school?
Second dinosaur: Reading, writhing, and arith-
metic.

First dinosaur: What famous baseball player
drives bugs batty?
Second dinosaur: Mickey Mantis!

First dinosaur: What do you call a bee that can't
make up his mind?
Second dinosaur: A maybee!

First dinosaur: What well-known cartoon char-
acter do moths like a lot?
Second dinosaur: Mickey Moth!

First dinosaur: How can you make a tarantula
shake?
Second dinosaur: Run up behind it and say,
"BOO!"

First dinosaur: Which bug does amazing motor-
cycle stunts?
Second dinosaur: Evel Boll Weevil!

First dinosaur: Which bug gobbles up trash?
Second dinosaur: The litterbug!

First dinosaur: How can you tell a male dinosaur
from a female dinosaur?
Second dinosaur: Ask it a question. If he answers,
it's a male; if she answers, it's a female.

First dinosaur: Where do cows go for lunch?
Second dinosaur: The calf-eteria.

First dinosaur: What do you call two spiders who
just got married?
Second dinosaur: Newlywebs.

First dinosaur: How do you burn a nitwit's ear?
Second dinosaur: Phone him while he's ironing.

First dinosaur: What do you get when you cross
a frog with a can of soda?
Second dinosaur: Croaka-Cola!

First dinosaur: What did the mountain say to the
earthquake?
Second dinosaur: It's not my fault!

First dinosaur: Why does the giraffe have such a
long neck?
Second dinosaur: His head is so far from his
body!

2

Dignified Dinosaurs

Q: What weighs 10,000 pounds, sits in a tree, and is very dangerous?
A: A dinosaur with a machine gun.

Q: What's gray and comes in ten-gallon jars?
A: Instant dinosaurs.

Q: Why did the dinosaur sit on the tomato?
A: He wanted to play squash.

Q: When is a dinosaur most likely to enter your house?
A: When the door is open.

Q: What's green on the inside and clear on the outside?
A: A dinosaur in a plastic bag.

Q: What color hair tint does a dinosaur use?
A: How should I know? Only her hairdresser knows for sure.

Q: What was the dinosaur doing in the road?
A: About two miles an hour.

Q: Why did the dinosaur wear green sneakers?
A: His blue ones were at the laundry.

Q: What's gray, weighs ten tons, and flies?
A: A dinosaur in a helicopter.

Q: What's red, blue, white, and orange?
A: A plaid dinosaur.

Q: How do you know when there's a dinosaur in your bed?
A: He has a "D" on his pajamas.

Q: What's the difference between a plum and a dinosaur?
A: One's purple and one's green.

Q: What's the best way to get something out from under a dinosaur?
A: Wait for the dinosaur to go away.

Q: What did the dinosaur say when the monkey stepped on his foot?
A: With tears in his eyes he said, "Why don't you pick on someone your own size?"

Q: Why did the dinosaur sit on a tack?
A: To see how high he could jump.

Q: Who started the dinosaur jokes?
A: That's what the dinosaurs would like to know.

Q: Did you hear about the man who shot a
   dinosaur in his pajamas?
A: The real question isn't whether you've heard
   about this, but how the dinosaur got into his
   pajamas.

Q: Why do dinosaurs step on lily pads?
A: The water won't hold them up.

Q: Why do dinosaurs clip their toenails?
A: So their ballet slippers will fit.

Q: What's green and lights up?
A: An electric dinosaur.

Q: What do you do when a dinosaur stubs his toe?
A: Call a very big toe truck.

Q: What did the plant-eating dinosaur say when winter ended and the trees sprouted new growth?
A: "Whew! That's a re-leaf!"

3

Dinosaur Knock, Knock Jokes

First dinosaur: Knock, knock.
Second dinosaur: Who's there?
First dinosaur: Donna.
Second dinosaur: Donna who?
First dinosaur: Donna keep me waiting out here!

First dinosaur: Knock, knock.
Second dinosaur: Who's there?
First dinosaur: Wendy.
Second dinosaur: Wendy who?
First dinosaur: Wendy door opens, I'll come in!

First dinosaur: Knock, knock.
Second dinosaur: Who's there?

First dinosaur: Elsie.
Second dinosaur: Elsie who?
First dinosaur: Elsie you in my dreams.

First dinosaur: Knock, knock.
Second dinosaur: Who's there?
First dinosaur: Celeste.
Second dinosaur: Celeste who?
First dinosaur: Celeste time I knock on this door!

First dinosaur: Knock, knock.
Second dinosaur: Who's there?
First dinosaur: Doris.
Second dinosaur: Doris who?
First dinosaur: Doris shut; that's why I'm
    knocking!

First dinosaur: Knock, knock.
Second dinosaur: Who's there?
First dinosaur: Yura.
Second dinosaur: Yura who?
First dinosaur: Yura best friend!

First dinosaur: Knock, knock.
Second dinosaur: Who's there?
First dinosaur: Carrot.
Second dinosaur: Carrot who?
First dinosaur: Carrot me back to old Virginia!

First dinosaur: Knock, knock.
Second dinosaur: Who's there?
First dinosaur: Castro.
Second dinosaur: Castro who?
First dinosaur: Castro bread upon the waters.

First dinosaur: Knock, knock.
Second dinosaur: Who's there?
First dinosaur: Toby.
Second dinosaur: Toby who?
First dinosaur: Toby or not to be, that is the question!

First dinosaur: Knock, knock.
Second dinosaur: Who's there?
First dinosaur: Iris.

Second dinosaur: Iris who?
First dinosaur: Iris I was rich!

First dinosaur: Knock, knock.
Second dinosaur: Who's there?
First dinosaur: Costa.
Second dinosaur: Costa who?
First dinosaur: Costa lot!

First dinosaur: Knock, knock.
Second dinosaur: Who's there?
First dinosaur: Iran.
Second dinosaur: Iran who?
First dinosaur: Iran over to see you!

First dinosaur: Knock, knock.
Second dinosaur: Who's there?
First dinosaur: Jess.
Second dinosaur: Jess who?
First dinosaur: Jess a friend of yours!

First dinosaur: Knock, knock.
Second dinosaur: Who's there?
First dinosaur: Missouri.
Second dinosaur: Missouri who?
First dinosaur: Missouri loves company!

First dinosaur: Knock, knock.
Second dinosaur: Who's there?
First dinosaur: Gravy.
Second dinosaur: Gravy who?
First dinosaur: Gravy Crockett!

First dinosaur: Knock, knock.
Second dinosaur: Who's there?
First dinosaur: Halibut.
Second dinosaur: Halibut who?
First dinosaur: Halibut a kiss, sweetie!

First dinosaur: Knock, knock.
Second dinosaur: Who's there?
First dinosaur: Congo.
Second dinosaur: Congo who?
First dinosaur: Congo out—I'm grounded!

First dinosaur: Knock, knock.
Second dinosaur: Who's there?
First dinosaur: Egypt.
Second dinosaur: Egypt who?
First dinosaur: Egypt me out of money!

First dinosaur: Knock, knock.
Second dinosaur: Who's there?
First dinosaur: Iowa.
Second dinosaur: Iowa who?
First dinosaur: Iowa you a dollar!

First dinosaur: Knock, knock.
Second dinosaur: Who's there?
First dinosaur: Havana.
Second dinosaur: Havana who?
First dinosaur: Havana good time?

First dinosaur: Knock, knock.
Second dinosaur: Who's there?
First dinosaur: Yukon.
Second dinosaur: Yukon who?
First dinosaur: Yukon let me in now!

First dinosaur: Knock, knock.
Second dinosaur: Who's there?
First dinosaur: Sam.
Second dinosaur: Sam who?
First dinosaur: Sam day my prince will come!

First dinosaur: Knock, knock.
Second dinosaur: Who's there?
First dinosaur: Woody.
Second dinosaur: Woody who?
First dinosaur: Woody ya open the door, please?

4

Delightful Dinosaurs

Q: What would happen if a dinosaur swallowed a frog?
A: It might croak.

Q: What weighs ten tons, has a long neck, and cuts through wood?
A: A dino-saw.

Q: What prehistoric animal spent most of its time talking?
A: The woolly mam-mouth.

Q: What do you call a dinosaur that's always walking in mud?
A: Brown-toe-saurus.

Q: Who was the scariest dinosaur of them all?
A: The terror-dactyl.

Q: Is it difficult to bury a dead dinosaur?
A: Yes, it's a huge undertaking.

Q: What's the difference between a world without prehistoric monsters and a room with no way out?
A: One has no dinosaurs, the other no sign o' doors.

Q: What do you do if a dinosaur sneezes?
A: Get out of the way!

Q: What kind of dinosaurs live in graveyards?
A: Cemetery-dactyls.

Q: What weighs ten tons and is bright red?
A: An embarrassed dinosaur.

Q: How do you tell a dinosaur from a banana?
A: Try lifting it. If you can't get it off the floor, it's probably a dinosaur. But it might be a heavy banana.

Q: What hangs on a tree and shouts "Help!"?
A: A dinosaur in distress.

Q: What's best for a blue dinosaur?
A: A trip to the circus to cheer him up.

Q: What do you give a seasick dinosaur?
A: Plenty of room.

Q: What was the dinosaur doing on the inter-
state?
A: About ten miles an hour.

Q: What's bright blue and weighs ten tons?
A: A dinosaur holding its breath.

Q: What did the apple say to the dinosaur?
A: Nothing. Apples can't talk.

Q: What's green, weighs ten tons, and leaves
footprints in the butter?
A: A dinosaur in the fridge.

Q: What's a dinosaur in a fridge called?
A: A very tight squeeze.

Q: What do dinosaurs say when they bump into
each other?
A: Small world, isn't it?

5

Dizzy Dinosaurs

Q: How do you shoot a white dinosaur?
A: You hold his nose until he turns blue, and then you shoot him with a blue dinosaur gun.

Q: What happens when you cross a dinosaur with a cow?
A: We don't know...but you have to stand up to milk it.

Q: Would you rather a dinosaur attacked you, or a gorilla?
A: I'd rather the dinosaur attacked the gorilla.

Q: Why is a dinosaur green, large, and wrinkled?
A: If he were small, white, and round, he would be an aspirin.

Q: What did the manta ray become when the dinosaur waded into the water and stepped on it?
A: An ex-ray.

Q: What time is it when a dinosaur sits on your car?
A: Time to get a new car.

Q: What do you get if you cross a spider with a dinosaur?
A: Who knows? But when it crawls across your ceiling, the roof will collapse!

Q: What's the difference between a dinosaur and an orange?
A: They're different colors.

Q: Why did the dinosaur stand on the marsh-
mallow?
A: So he wouldn't fall into the cocoa.

Q: What's red, blue, yellow, green, orange,
purple, and gray?
A: A Madrassaur.

Q: How do you stop a dinosaur from sticking his
head out the backseat window?
A: Make him sit up front.

Q: What is the best way to cure a dinosaur who
walks in his sleep?
A: Put tacks on the floor.

Q: Why do dinosaurs eat raw meat?
A: They don't know how to cook.

Q: What does an electric dinosaur say?
A: Watts up, Doc?

Q: Why did the dinosaur paint himself all different colors?
A: So he could hide in the crayon box.

Q: How can you tell a dinosaur from spaghetti?
A: The dinosaur doesn't slip off the end of your fork.

Q: How do you make a dinosaur stew?
A: Keep it waiting for two hours.

6

The Dinosaur Freeway

First dinosaur: How do you keep a dog from crossing the road?
Second dinosaur: You put him in a barking lot.

First dinosaur: Why did the pigs cross the road with their laundry?
Second dinosaur: They wanted to do their hog-wash.

First dinosaur: Did you hear about the two kangaroos who crossed the road?
Second dinosaur: They jumped into each other's pouches and were never seen again.

First dinosaur: Why did the one-handed gorilla
cross the road?
Second dinosaur: To get to the second-hand shop.

First dinosaur: What do you call a chicken that
crosses the road without looking both ways?
Second dinosaur: Dead.

First dinosaur: What do you get if you cross the
road with a bear and a skunk?
Second dinosaur: Winnie-the-Phew.

First dinosaur: Why did the rabbit cross the road?
Second dinosaur: To get to the hopping mall.

First dinosaur: Why did the wasp cross the road?
Second dinosaur: It needed to go to the wasp-ital.

First dinosaur: Why did the hen go halfway
    across the road and stop?
Second dinosaur: She wanted to lay it on the line.

First dinosaur: Why did the sheep cross the road?
Second dinosaur: He needed to go to the baa-baa
    shop.

First dinosaur: Why did the otter cross the road?
Second dinosaur: To get to the otter side.

First dinosaur: Why did the elephant cross the
    road?
Second dinosaur: To pick up the squashed
    chicken.

First dinosaur: Why did the sick rabbits cross the
    road?
Second dinosaur: They needed to go to the
    hop-ital.

First dinosaur: What was the farmer doing on the other side of the road?
Second dinosaur: Catching all the chickens who tried to cross the road.

First dinosaur: Why do skunks always argue when crossing the road?
Second dinosaur: They like to raise a stink.

First dinosaur: What well-known animal crosses the road and drives all over the road?
Second dinosaur: A road hog.

First dinosaur: Why did the turkey cross the road?
Second dinosaur: It was the chicken's day off.

First dinosaur: Why did the chicken cross the road to the playground?
Second dinosaur: To get to the other slide.

First dinosaur: Where do animals go when they lose their tails?
Second dinosaur: They go across the road to the retail shop.

First dinosaur: Why did the duck cross the road?
Second dinosaur: The chicken retired and moved to Florida.

First dinosaur: Why did the chicken cross the muddy road and not come back?
Second dinosaur: He didn't want to be a dirty double-crosser!

First dinosaur: Why did the goose cross the road?
Second dinosaur: The light was green.

First dinosaur: Why did the hen cross the street?
Second dinosaur: To see a man lay bricks.

First dinosaur: Why did the cow cross the road?
Second dinosaur: To see its fodder.

First dinosaur: Did you hear the story about the
    peacock who crossed the road?
Second dinosaur: It is really a colorful tale…

First dinosaur: Why did the turtle cross the road?
Second dinosaur: To get to the Shell station.

First dinosaur: Why did the rooster cross the
    street?
Second dinosaur: To get to the other side.

7

More Knock, Knock Jokes

First dinosaur: Knock, knock.
Second dinosaur: Who's there?
First dinosaur: Oscar.
Second dinosaur: Oscar who?
First dinosaur: Oscar for a date!

First dinosaur: Knock, knock.
Second dinosaur: Who's there?
First dinosaur: Willie.
Second dinosaur: Willie who?
First dinosaur: Willie be home for dinner?

First dinosaur: Knock, knock.
Second dinosaur: Who's there?
First dinosaur: Hans.
Second dinosaur: Hans who?
First dinosaur: Hans off the table!

First dinosaur: Knock, knock.
Second dinosaur: Who's there?
First dinosaur: Theodore.
Second dinosaur: Theodore who?
First dinosaur: Theodore is shut!

First dinosaur: Knock, knock.
Second dinosaur: Who's there?
First dinosaur: Isadore.
Second dinosaur: Isadore who?
First dinosaur: Isadore necessary?

First dinosaur: Knock, knock.
Second dinosaur: Who's there?
First dinosaur: Raymond.
Second dinosaur: Raymond who?
First dinosaur: Raymond me to buy milk!

First dinosaur: Knock, knock.
Second dinosaur: Who's there?
First dinosaur: Walter.
Second dinosaur: Walter who?
First dinosaur: Walter wall carpeting!

First dinosaur: Knock, knock.
Second dinosaur: Who's there?
First dinosaur: Martha.
Second dinosaur: Martha who?
First dinosaur: Martha right here and open the
    door!

First dinosaur: Knock, knock.
Second dinosaur: Who's there?
First dinosaur: Althea.
Second dinosaur: Althea who?
First dinosaur: Althea later, alligator!

First dinosaur: Knock, knock.
Second dinosaur: Who's there?
First dinosaur: Willa.
Second dinosaur: Willa who?
First dinosaur: Willa you go on a date with me?

First dinosaur: Knock, knock.
Second dinosaur: Who's there?
First dinosaur: Henrietta.
Second dinosaur: Henrietta who?
First dinosaur: Henrietta the dessert.

First dinosaur: Knock, knock.
Second dinosaur: Who's there?
First dinosaur: Jewel.
Second dinosaur: Jewel who?
First dinosaur: Jewel know who when you open
the door.

First dinosaur: Knock, knock.
Second dinosaur: Who's there?
First dinosaur: Harriet.
Second dinosaur: Harriet who?
First dinosaur: Harriet up and open the door!

First dinosaur: Knock, knock.
Second dinosaur: Who's there?
First dinosaur: Frank.
Second dinosaur: Frank who?
First dinosaur: Frank and beans.

First dinosaur: Knock, knock.
Second dinosaur: Who's there?
First dinosaur: Ken.

Second dinosaur: Ken who?
First dinosaur: Ken you see me?

First dinosaur: Knock, knock.
Second dinosaur: Who's there?
First dinosaur: Arnold.
Second dinosaur: Arnold who?
First dinosaur: Arnold you tired of all these
    knock, knock jokes?

First dinosaur: Knock, knock.
Second dinosaur: Who's there?
First dinosaur: Lenny.
Second dinosaur: Lenny who?
First dinosaur: Lenny in; I'm cold out here!

First dinosaur: Knock, knock.
Second dinosaur: Who's there?
First dinosaur: Lemon.
Second dinosaur: Lemon who?
First dinosaur: Lemon me give you a kiss!

First dinosaur: Knock, knock.
Second dinosaur: Who's there?
First dinosaur: Randy.
Second dinosaur: Randy who?
First dinosaur: Randy four-minute mile!

First dinosaur: Knock, knock.
Second dinosaur: Who's there?
First dinosaur: Chuck.
Second dinosaur: Chuck who?
First dinosaur: Chuck and see if the door is
    unlocked.

8

Distinguished Dinosaurs

Q: What does a dinosaur become after it's 49
   years old?
A: Fifty years old.

Q: Is it true that a dinosaur won't attack you if
   you carry a flashlight?
A: That depends on how fast you carry it.

Q: What is green and has 16 wheels?
A: A dinosaur on roller skates.

Q: How do you run over a dinosaur?
A: Climb up its tail, dash toward its head, and
   slide down its neck.

Q: What's big, fierce, and is worn around your neck?
A: A tie-rannosaurus.

Q: What do you call a dinosaur that steps on everything in its way?
A: Tyrannosaurus wrecks.

Q: What do you call a dinosaur in a hurry?
A: A prontosaurus.

Q: What's green, weighs ten tons, and plays squash?
A: A dinosaur in a phone booth.

Q: What did one dinosaur say to the other?
A: Nothing! Dinosaurs can't talk! They only whistle.

Q: Why do dinosaurs have sore ankles?
A: From wearing their sneakers too tight!

Q: Why do ducks have webbed feet?
A: To stamp out forest fires!

Q: Why do dinosaurs have flat feet?
A: To stamp out burning ducks!

Q: Why do dinosaurs wear blue sneakers?
A: Their yellow ones are not in style!

Q: How does a dinosaur get in a tree?
A: He hides in an acorn and waits for a squirrel
   to carry him up!

Q: Why do girl dinosaurs wear angora sweaters?
A: So you can tell them apart from boy
   dinosaurs!

Q: What is the most dangerous thing for
   dinosaurs with long tails?
A: Getting them caught in subway doors!

Q: Why do dinosaurs live in jungles?
A: It's away from the high-rent district!

Q: Why do dinosaurs climb up palm trees?
A: To try out their new sneakers!

Q: Why don't dinosaurs go to college?
A: a. They don't fit through the entrance door!
    b. They didn't finish high school!
    c. There are no colleges in the jungle!

Q: What's the similarity between a plum and a
   dinosaur?
A: They're both purple, except for the dinosaur.

9

Ding-a-Ling Dinosaur Jokes

First dinosaur: Which is the dumbest ant?
Second dinosaur: Ignor*ant!*

First dinosaur: How do bees make money?
Second dinosaur: They cell their honey!

First dinosaur: How do robins get in shape?
Second dinosaur: They do worm-ups.

First dinosaur: Who gets paid for never doing a
     day's work?
Second dinosaur: A night watchman.

First dinosaur: Is writing on an empty stomach harmful?
Second dinosaur: No, but paper is better.

First dinosaur: How can you get into a locked house, with all the windows tightly barred, without a key?
Second dinosaur: Keep running around the house until you're all in.

First dinosaur: What do you call a rabbit who has never been out of the house?
Second dinosaur: An ingrown hare.

First dinosaur: When does a caterpillar improve its morals?
Second dinosaur: When it turns over a new leaf.

First dinosaur: What should a man know before trying to teach a dog?
Second dinosaur: More than the dog.

First dinosaur: Imagine you were in the jungle and were being chased by a woolly mammoth. What would you do?
Second dinosaur: I would stop imagining!

First dinosaur: How do you get a woolly mammoth out of a bathtub?
Second dinosaur: Pull out the plug.

First dinosaur: What's the highest form of animal life?
Second dinosaur: The giraffe.

First dinosaur: Why did Grandpa Flintstone order chicken for dinner?
Second dinosaur: He was in a fowl mood.

First dinosaur: Why was the little mosquito up so late?
Second dinosaur: He had to study for his blood test!

First dinosaur: How can you tell which end of a worm is its head?
Second dinosaur: I have no clue.
First dinosaur: Tell it a joke, and see which end laughs.

First dinosaur: What do you get from petting rabbits with sharp teeth?
Second dinosaur: Beats me.
First dinosaur: Hare cuts.

First dinosaur: What do you call a boy who sticks his right arm down a lion's throat?
Second dinosaur: I can't guess.
First dinosaur: Lefty.

First dinosaur: What do you get when you cross
a tiger and a parrot?
Second dinosaur: I have no idea.
First dinosaur: I don't know, but when it asks for
a cracker, you better give it one!

First dinosaur: Why did the farmer wash the
chicken's mouth out with soap?
Second dinosaur: You tell me.
First dinosaur: It was using fowl language.

First dinosaur: What's gray, weighs five tons, and
wears glass slippers?
Second dinosaur: I give up.
First dinosaur: Cinderelephant.

First dinosaur: What would you call a prehistoric
skunk?
Second dinosaur: Who knows?
First dinosaur: Ex-stinct.

Deep in the jungle, a trio of animals were discussing who among them was the most powerful.

"I am," said the hawk, "because I can fly and swoop down swiftly at my prey."

"I am," said the mountain lion, "because I am not only fleet, but I have powerful teeth and claws."

"I am," said the skunk, "because with a flick of my tail, I can drive off the two of you."

Suddenly a huge dinosaur lumbered over and settled the debate by eating them all, hawk, lion, and stinker.

First dinosaur: How do you treat a pig with a
    sore throat?
Second dinosaur: You've got me.
First dinosaur: Apply oinkment.

First dinosaur: What do you call a camel without
    a hump?
Second dinosaur: That's a mystery.
First dinosaur: Humphrey.

First dinosaur: Did you hear the one about the snake who had an extra job on rainy days?
Second dinosaur: I'm blank.
First dinosaur: He was a windshield viper.

First dinosaur: What would you get if you crossed a flea with a rabbit?
Second dinosaur: I don't have the foggiest.
First dinosaur: A bug's bunny.

First dinosaur: Which is less intelligent—a large chicken or a small chicken?
Second dinosaur: It's unknown to me.
First dinosaur: The large one is the bigger cluck.

First dinosaur: What is the best way to hold a bat?
Second dinosaur: I'm in the dark.
First dinosaur: By the wings.

First dinosaur: What is a ringleader?
Second dinosaur: You've got me guessing.
First dinosaur: The first person in the bathtub.

First dinosaur: What do you get when you cross a chicken with a construction worker?
Second dinosaur: I pass.
First dinosaur: A bricklayer.

First dinosaur: Why is a pig in the house like a house afire?
Second dinosaur: How should I know?
First dinosaur: The sooner you put it out, the better.

First dinosaur: What did Hannibal get when he crossed the Alps with elephants?
Second dinosaur: Beats me.
First dinosaur: Mountains that never forget.

First dinosaur: What is yellow, smooth, and very
    dangerous?
Second dinosaur: I can't guess.
First dinosaur: Shark-infested custard.

10

Dynamic Dinosaurs

Customer: Your sign says, "$50 to anyone who orders something we can't furnish." I would like to have a dinosaur-ear sandwich.

Waiter: Ohhh…we're going to have to pay you the $50.

Customer: No dinosaur ears, huh?

Waiter: Oh, we've got lots of them…but we're all out of those big buns!

Q: What kind of eggs does a wicked dinosaur lay?
A: Deviled eggs.

Q: What do you get if you cross a dinosaur with a Boy Scout?
A: A dinosaur that helps old ladies cross the street.

Q: What is the best thing to take when you're run over by a dinosaur?
A: The license number of the car that hit you.

Q: What did the dinosaur say when it was put in the pot?
A: Boy, am I in hot water!

Q: Why do dinosaurs wear sneakers while jumping from tree to tree?
A: a. So they won't get their feet dirty!
   b. So they don't get splinters!
   c. So they won't wake up their neighbors!

Q: Why do dinosaurs wear sunglasses?
A: a. To make themselves look glamorous!
   b. So Tarzan won't recognize them!
   c. So they don't step on other dinosaurs!
   d. To cover their baggy eyes!

Q: What did the dinosaurs say when they saw
Charles de Gaulle?
A: a. Voilà le Charles de Gaulle!
b. Nothing…dinosaurs can't speak French!
c. Say hello to our French relatives!

Q: Why did the dinosaur wear sunglasses?
A: With all the silly dinosaur riddles around, he
didn't want to be recognized.

Q: What would you get if Batman and Robin
were run over by a herd of stampeding
dinosaurs?
A: Flatman and Ribbon.

Q: When does a mouse weigh as much as a
dinosaur?
A: When the scale is broken.

Q: If you were in a jungle by yourself and a
dinosaur charged you, what would you do?
A: Pay him.

Q: If there were three dinosaurs in a kitchen,
   which one would be a cowboy?
A: The one on the range.

Q: What did the dinosaur think of the grape's
   house?
A: Di-vine.

Q: If a dinosaur were eating your book, what
   would you do?
A: I would take the words right out of his mouth.

Q: What's the difference between a dinosaur and
   a coconut?
A: Coconuts hang in trees.

Q: What's green and stamps out jungle fires?
A: Smokey the dinosaur.

Q: How can you tell if there is a dinosaur in the refrigerator?
A: The door won't shut.

Q: Why is a dinosaur green?
A: He has iron-poor blood.

Q: How do you lift a dinosaur?
A: Put him on an acorn and let it grow.

Still More
Knock, Knock Jokes

First dinosaur: Knock, knock.
Second dinosaur: Who's there?
First dinosaur: Watson.
Second dinosaur: Watson who?
First dinosaur: Nothing much. Watsonew with
    you?

First dinosaur: Knock, knock.
Second dinosaur: Who's there?
First dinosaur: Mecca.
Second dinosaur: Mecca who?
First dinosaur: Mecca me happy!

First dinosaur: Knock, knock.
Second dinosaur: Who's there?
First dinosaur: Betty.
Second dinosaur: Betty who?
First dinosaur: Betty ya don't know who this is!

First dinosaur: Knock, knock.
Second dinosaur: Who's there?
First dinosaur: Gladys.
Second dinosaur: Gladys who?
First dinosaur: Gladys my last knock, knock joke!

First dinosaur: Knock, knock.
Second dinosaur: Who's there?
First dinosaur: Mae.
Second dinosaur: Mae who?
First dinosaur: Mae be I'll tell you and maybe I
    won't!

First dinosaur: Knock, knock.
Second dinosaur: Who's there?
First dinosaur: Abbott.
Second dinosaur: Abbott who?
First dinosaur: Abbott time you answered the
    door.

First dinosaur: Knock, knock.
Second dinosaur: Who's there?
First dinosaur: Jilly.
Second dinosaur: Jilly who?
First dinosaur: Jilly out here and I'm freezing.
    Can I come in?

First dinosaur: Knock, knock.
Second dinosaur: Who's there?
First dinosaur: Phyllis.
Second dinosaur: Phyllis who?
First dinosaur: Phyllis glass up with Coke please,
    I'm thirsty!

First dinosaur: Knock, knock.
Second dinosaur: Who's there?
First dinosaur: Emma.
Second dinosaur: Emma who?
First dinosaur: Emma tired, are you tired, too?

First dinosaur: Knock, knock.
Second dinosaur: Who's there?
First dinosaur: Marietta.
Second dinosaur: Marietta who?
First dinosaur: Marietta the whole bowl of pop-
    corn.

First dinosaur: Knock, knock.
Second dinosaur: Who's there?
First dinosaur: Paula.
Second dinosaur: Paula who?
First dinosaur: Paula the handle; the door is open.

First dinosaur: Knock, knock.
Second dinosaur: Who's there?
First dinosaur: Denise.
Second dinosaur: Denise who?
First dinosaur: Denise are connected to your legs.

First dinosaur: Knock, knock.
Second dinosaur: Who's there?
First dinosaur: Sue.
Second dinosaur: Sue who?
First dinosaur: Sue whomever you want; I didn't
    break your doorbell.

First dinosaur: Knock, knock.
Second dinosaur: Who's there?
First dinosaur: Joan.
Second dinosaur: Joan who?
First dinosaur: Joan't you know who's knocking?

First dinosaur: Knock, knock.
Second dinosaur: Who's there?
First dinosaur: Ida.
Second dinosaur: Ida who?
First dinosaur: Ida want to stand outside all night!

First dinosaur: Knock, knock.
Second dinosaur: Who's there?
First dinosaur: Lily.
Second dinosaur: Lily who?
First dinosaur: Lily House on the Prairie!

First dinosaur: Knock, knock.
Second dinosaur: Who's there?
First dinosaur: Shirley.
Second dinosaur: Shirley who?
First dinosaur: Shirley, you're going to open the door.

First dinosaur: Knock, knock.
Second dinosaur: Who's there?
First dinosaur: Carrie.
Second dinosaur: Carrie who?
First dinosaur: Carrie me back to bed; I'm tired.

First dinosaur: Knock, knock.
Second dinosaur: Who's there?
First dinosaur: Verdi.
Second dinosaur: Verdi who?
First dinosaur: Verdi been all day?

First dinosaur: Knock, knock.
Second dinosaur: Who's there?
First dinosaur: Albee.
Second dinosaur: Albee who?
First dinosaur: Albee a monkey's uncle!

First dinosaur: Knock, knock.
Second dinosaur: Who's there?
First dinosaur: Gable.
Second dinosaur: Gable who?
First dinosaur: Gable to leap tall buildings in a
    single bound!

12

Dashing Dinosaurs

Q: What's the difference between a loaf of bread and a dinosaur?
A: Well, if you don't know the difference, I'm certainly not going to send you to the store for a loaf of bread!

Q: Why can't dinosaurs hitchhike?
A: They don't have thumbs!

Q: Why do dinosaurs roll down the hill?
A: They can't roll up very well!

Q: How do you know when there's a dinosaur in your bathtub?
A: You can smell the onions on his breath.

Q: Where do you find dinosaurs?
A: It depends on where you leave them!

Q: Why do dinosaurs catch colds?
A: You would too if you ran around without any
   clothes on!

Q: What do you find between dinosaurs' toes?
A: Slow-running dinosaur hunters!

Q: Why do dinosaurs wear yellow caps?
A: So they can tiptoe across a pool table without
   being seen!

Q: What's the worst part of eating dinosaur?
A: You have leftovers for weeks and weeks!

Q: How do you greet a two-headed dinosaur?
A: Hello! Hello!

Q: How do we know the age of dinosaurs?
A: By going to their birthday parties!

Q: Why did dinosaurs' teeth keep falling out?
A: Who knows—maybe they'd have stayed in
   longer if fluoride toothpaste had been around!

Q: How did the dinosaur go on a diet?
A: It ate a cottage-cheese factory!

Q: What did the dinosaur eat?
A: Anything it wanted!

Q: What do you do with a green dinosaur?
A: Wait until it ripens.

Q: Do dinosaurs make good house pets?
A: Only if they are housebroken!

13

More Ding-a-Ling Dinosaur Jokes

First dinosaur: Why did the little girl take hay to bed?
Second dinosaur: To feed her nightmare.

First dinosaur: Why did the rabbit go to the doctor?
Second dinosaur: He felt jumpy!

First dinosaur: What happened to the two bed-bugs who fell in love?
Second dinosaur: They were married in the spring!

First dinosaur: Why can't you tell secrets on a farm?
Second dinosaur: The corn has ears, the potatoes have eyes, the grass whispers, and the horses carry tails.

First dinosaur: What did the Cinderella fish wear to the ball?
Second dinosaur: Glass flippers.

First dinosaur: What's smarter than a talking horse?
Second dinosaur: A spelling bee.

First dinosaur: What did the duck say when it laid a square egg?
Second dinosaur: Ouch!

First dinosaur: When is it socially correct to serve milk in a saucer?
Second dinosaur: When you're feeding the cat.

First dinosaur: How do you tell the difference between an elephant and a rhinoceros?
Second dinosaur: The elephant has a better memory.

First dinosaur: What does a frog say when it washes car windows?
Second dinosaur: Rub it, rub it, rub it.

First dinosaur: What has feathers and writes?
Second dinosaur: A ballpoint hen.

First dinosaur: Which is the bossiest ant?
Second dinosaur: Tyr*ant!*

First dinosaur: What do moose do at a concert?
Second dinosaur: Make moosic.

First dinosaur: What do you call it when giraffes
moving one way get mixed-up with giraffes
moving another way?
Second dinosaur: A giraffic jam.

First dinosaur: If you were surrounded by 30
lions, 25 elephants, and 10 hippos, how
would you get away from them?
Second dinosaur: Step off the merry-go-round.

First dinosaur: Which ant is an army soldier?
Second dinosaur: Serge*ant!*

First dinosaur: What do monkeys eat for dessert?
Second dinosaur: Chocolate chimp cookies.

14

Daffy Dinosaurs

First dinosaur: Do you like my new dress? I got it
for a ridiculous price!
Second dinosaur: You mean you got it for an
absurd figure?

First dinosaur: What do you call a cat who drinks
lemonade?
Second dinosaur: Beats me.
First dinosaur: A sourpuss.

First dinosaur: What do you call a sleeping bull?
Second dinosaur: I can't guess.
First dinosaur: A bulldozer.

First dinosaur: What is worse than a giraffe with a sore throat?
Second dinosaur: I have no idea.
First dinosaur: A centipede with corns.

First dinosaur: What does a dog make his clothes out of?
Second dinosaur: I give up.
First dinosaur: Mutt-erial.

First dinosaur: Did you know that a grasshopper can jump four times its own length and sometimes even more?
Second dinosaur: Yeah, but once I saw a hornet lift a two-hundred-pound man one foot off the ground.

First dinosaur: What kind of teeth can you buy for a dollar?
Second dinosaur: Who knows?
First dinosaur: Buck teeth.

First dinosaur: What's worse than a hoarse horse?
Second dinosaur: You've got me.
First dinosaur: A chicken chicken.

First dinosaur: Why did the farmer name his hog Ink?
Second dinosaur: My mind is a blank.
First dinosaur: Because he was always running out of his pen.

First dinosaur: What has two heads, one tail, four legs on one side, and two legs on the other?
Second dinosaur: That's a mystery.
First dinosaur: A horse with a lady riding sidesaddle.

First dinosaur: How does a skunk defend itself?
Second dinosaur: I'm blank.
First dinosaur: Instinct.

First dinosaur: How does a farmer take a sick pig
to the hospital?
Second dinosaur: I don't have the foggiest.
First dinosaur: In a hambulance.

First dinosaur: Why was the baby chicken
thrown out of school?
Second dinosaur: It's unknown to me.
First dinosaur: It was caught peeping during a
test.

First dinosaur: What has 20 sharp teeth, a 90-foot
tail, and scales all over it?
Second dinosaur: I'm in the dark.
First dinosaur: I don't know, but you'd better run
if you see one!

First dinosaur: What has an elephant's trunk, a
giraffe's neck, a bird's beak, and a lion's
head?
Second dinosaur: Search me.
First dinosaur: A zoo.

First dinosaur: Why does a man who has just
shaved look like a wild animal?
Second dinosaur: You've got me guessing.
First dinosaur: He has a bear face.

First dinosaur: What did the leopard say when he
finished the hot dog?
Second dinosaur: I pass.
First dinosaur: That hit the spot.

First dinosaur: Ten cats were in a boat. One
jumped out. How many were left?
Second dinosaur: Nine.
First dinosaur: Wrong—none were left. All the
rest were copycats.

First dinosaur: What animal has two humps and
is found in Alaska?
Second dinosaur: How should I know?
First dinosaur: A lost camel.

First dinosaur: What's all muddy and goes
    around on Easter passing out eggs?
Second dinosaur: I don't know.
First dinosaur: The Easter Pig.

First dinosaur: What is the best way to talk to a
    hot dog?
Second dinosaur: I have no clue.
First dinosaur: Be frank.

More Dynamic Dinosaurs

First dinosaur: I feel like a trash can!
Second dinosaur: Rubbish!

First dinosaur: You must do something for me. I
    snore so loudly, I wake myself up.
Second dinosaur: In that case, I would advise you
    to sleep in another room.

First dinosaur: The woolly mammoths helped to
    improve the neighborhood.
Second dinosaur: How'd they do that?
First dinosaur: They moved.

82

First dinosaur: Do you want to hear a joke about bowling?
Second dinosaur: Spare me!

First dinosaur: I always do my hardest work before breakfast.
Second dinosaur: What is that?
First dinosaur: Getting up.

First dinosaur: Is it difficult to become a professional puppeteer?
Second dinosaur: Well, you'll have to pull a lot of strings.

First dinosaur: Did you ever try to tickle a mule?
Second dinosaur: No. Why?
First dinosaur: You'd get a big kick out of it!

First dinosaur: I once had to live on a can of beans for a whole week.
Second dinosaur: My goodness! Weren't you afraid of falling off?

First dinosaur: Your alarm clock was ringing
   about an hour ago.
Second dinosaur: Well, why didn't you tell me
   then?
First dinosaur: You were asleep!

First dinosaur: I can't get this match to light.
Second dinosaur: Why, what's wrong with it?
First dinosaur: Don't know. It worked all right
   yesterday.

First dinosaur: I'm exhausted! I was up until
   midnight doing homework!
Second dinosaur: What time did you start?
First dinosaur: Eleven forty-five.

First dinosaur: I can imitate any bird.
Second dinosaur: How about a homing pigeon?

84

First dinosaur: It'll be your birthday soon. How would you like to have a pocket calculator?
Second dinosaur: No, thanks. I already know how many pockets I have.

First dinosaur: Are you getting a new hairdo for the party?
Second dinosaur: No, I'm having a henna-do.
First dinosaur: What's a henna-do?
Second dinosaur: It runs around and says, "Cluck, cluck!"

First dinosaur: How did you make this cake?
Second dinosaur: Here's the recipe. I cut it out of a magazine.
First dinosaur: Are you sure you read the right page? The other side tells how to make a rock garden.

First dinosaur: When I grow up, I want to be a millionaire. I'll have a great big house with no bathrooms.
Second dinosaur: Why no bathrooms?
First dinosaur: I'm going to be filthy rich!

First dinosaur: Have you given the goldfish fresh water today?
Second dinosaur: No, he hasn't drunk what I gave him yesterday.

16

Dinky Dinosaurs

Q: How can you tell when there is a dinosaur under your bed?
A: When you wake up, you are nearly touching the ceiling.

Q: What do you get when you cross a saber-toothed tiger with a dinosaur?
A: A nervous mailman.

Q: What's the best way to raise a dinosaur?
A: Use a crane.

Fred: Why do dinosaurs paint their toenails all
    different colors?
Barney: So they can hide in jelly bean jars.
Fred: I've never seen a dinosaur in a jelly bean
    jar!
Barney: See how good they hide?

Q: What do you call a prehistoric animal the day
    after it's exercised much too much?
A: A dinosore.

Q: Why do dinosaurs lie down?
A: They can't lie up.

While taking a long drink at a pond, a
dinosaur happened to glance up and spotted a
snapping turtle lying on a nearby stone. Its eyes
narrowing, the dinosaur lumbered over, raised a
foot, and pressed the turtle flat.

Observing the murder from the jungle, a
zebra wandered over.

"Why the heck did you do that?"

"This was the same animal that bit off the tip
of my nose over ten years ago."

The zebra's eyes widened. "The same one? You must have an incredible memory!"

Raising its head proudly, the dinosaur said, "Turtle recall."

Q: Which dinosaurs don't get cavities?
A: Those in the half of the herd that use Crest.

Q: If 20 dinosaurs run after one of the Flintstones, what time is it?
A: Twenty after one.

First dinosaur: Have you ever seen a dinosaur hide?
Second dinosaur: No.
First dinosaur: They hide pretty well, don't they?

Q: What was the dinosaur doing on the road?
A: Trying to trip the ants.

Q: Why did the dinosaur cross the road?
A: To prove he wasn't chicken.

Q: How do you make a dinosaur sandwich?
A: First of all you get a very large loaf of bread...

Q: What's as big as a dinosaur and doesn't weigh anything?
A: A dinosaur's shadow.

Q: Why did the dinosaur lie in the road with his feet in the air?
A: He wanted to trip the birds.

Q: If a dinosaur was on a leaf in a tree, how would it get down?
A: It would wait for autumn.

Q: How do you make a slow dinosaur fast?
A: Don't feed him!

Q: What's the difference between a girl dinosaur
and a boy dinosaur?
A: One sings soprano, one sings bass!

Q: Why do dinosaurs never lie?
A: The ground isn't very comfortable!

Q: What's green and red all over?
A: A sunburned dinosaur!

Q: When you buy dinosaurs, what should you
always check for first?
A: The Good Housekeeping Seal of Approval!

Woolly Mammoths

Q: What words do you use to scold a woolly mammoth?
A: Tusk, tusk!

Q: Why does a woolly mammoth have a trunk?
A: He'd look pretty silly with a glove compartment.

Q: Which takes longer to get ready for a trip—a rooster or a woolly mammoth?
A: The woolly mammoth—he has to take a trunk while the rooster takes only his comb.

Q: What has two tails, six feet, and two trunks?
A: A woolly mammoth with spare parts.

Q: Why do woolly mammoths have trunks?
A: They'd look silly with suitcases, wouldn't they?

Q: How can you tell if there is a woolly mammoth in your sleeping bag?
A: By the smell of peanuts on his breath.

Q: Why wasn't the woolly mammoth allowed on the plane?
A: His trunk wouldn't fit under the seat.

Q: Why did the woolly mammoth take two trunks on his vacation?
A: One to drink through and the other to swim in.

Q: Why do woolly mammoths' tusks stick out?
A: Their parents couldn't afford braces.

Q: Why do woolly mammoths have squinting eyes?
A: From reading the small print on peanut packages!

Q: Why are woolly mammoths' tusks easier to find in Alabama?
A: Because their "Tuscaloosa."

Q: Why does a woolly mammoth have a trunk?
A: To hide himself when he sees a mouse!

Q: Why do woolly mammoths have white tusks?
A: They use the Crest Formula!

Q: Why do woolly mammoths have trunks?
A: They don't have pockets to put things in.

Q: Why did the woolly mammoth swallow a
   camphor ball?
A: To keep moths out of his trunk.

Q: Why do woolly mammoths carry keys?
A: To open their trunks.

Q: How can you tell there's a woolly mammoth
   on your back during a storm?
A: You can hear his ears flapping.

18

Delicate Dinosaurs

Q: Why do dinosaurs have toenails?
A: So they can have something to chew!

Q: What's white on the outside, green in the
middle, and heavy in your stomach?
A: A dinosaur sandwich.

Q: What's pink, slimy, and weighs ten tons?
A: An inside out dinosaur.

Q: What's green, weighs ten tons, and jumps
higher than a house?
A: A dinosaur! Houses can't jump.

Q: What's red, weighs ten tons, and sits in a cherry tree?
A: A dinosaur disguised as a cherry.

Q: What goes "Clomp, clomp, clomp, swish—clomp, clomp, clomp, swish"?
A: A dinosaur with one wet tennis shoe.

Q: Why are dinosaurs bad dancers?
A: They have two left feet.

Q: When the biggest dinosaur in the world fell into a 30-foot well, how did they get it out?
A: Wet.

Q: Why is a dinosaur green?
A: So you won't mistake him for a bluebird.

Q: What do you get when you cross a parrot with a dinosaur?
A: A ten-ton bird that eats peanuts.

Q: What is the difference between a dinosaur and a blueberry?
A: A blueberry is blue.

Fred: I wish I had enough money to buy a dinosaur.
Barney: Why on earth do you want a dinosaur?
Fred: I don't. I just want the money.

Q: What do you get if you cross a canary and a dinosaur?
A: A pretty messy cage.

Q: What would you get if you crossed a skunk and a dinosaur?
A: A dirty look from the dinosaur.

Q: How do you make a pickle laugh?
A: Tell it a dinosaur joke.

Q: How do you get a dinosaur out of the theater?
A: You can't. It's in their blood.

Dinosaurs' Daffy Dictionary

19

Appetizers: Little things you keep eating until you've lost your appetite.

Astronomer: A night watchman.

Bank: A place that will lend you money if you can prove you don't need it.

Children: Small people who are not permitted to act the way their parents did at that age.

Copper Ore: Something used to paddle a copper boat.

Cough: Something you yourself can't help, but which everyone else does to annoy you.

Dream Girl: One who costs twice as much as you dreamed she would.

Driving: If your wife wants to learn to drive, don't stand in her way.

Dry Dock: A thirsty physician.

Duty: Something one looks forward to without pleasure, does with reluctance, and boasts about afterwards.

Editor: A literary barber.

Eiffel Tower: The Empire State Building, after taxes.

Elevator: It has its ups and downs.

Friendliness: Some folks make you feel at home. Others make you wish you were.

Gentleman: A true gentleman is a man who knows how to play the bagpipes, but doesn't.

Geologist: A fault finder.

Golf: A long walk punctuated with disappointments.

Grudge: A place to keep an automobile.

Housework: Something a woman does, but which no one notices—until she doesn't do it.

Insurance: Something that keeps you poor all your life so that you can die rich.

Joint Account: Something that is never over-drawn by the wife, just under-deposited by the husband.

Luck: I'm so unlucky that if ever my ship comes in, there will probably be a dock strike on.

Memory: The diary we all carry about with us.

Nursery School: A place where they teach those who hit, not to hit—and those that don't hit, to hit back.

Optician: Someone who helps you look better.

Pollution: Grime in the streets.

Race Horse: The only creature that can take thousands of people for a ride at the same time.

Recession: A period when we have to go without things our grandparents never heard of.

Satellite: Something to put on a horse if you're riding at night.

Speed: Every time I start thinking that the world is moving too fast, I go to the post office.

Television: An electric device which, when broken, stimulates conversation.

More Distinguished Dinosaurs

First dinosaur: How can you get a set of teeth put in for free?
Second dinosaur: I have no clue.
First dinosaur: Kick a saber-toothed tiger.

First dinosaur: Where do young cows go to dance?
Second dinosaur: I can't guess.
First dinosaur: To the dis-cow-teque.

First dinosaur: When do pigs give their girl-friends presents?
Second dinosaur: I have no idea.
First dinosaur: On Valen-swine's Day.

First dinosaur: What is a sick crocodile?
Second dinosaur: You tell me.
First dinosaur: An illigator.

First dinosaur: What kind of pickle does a dentist use?
Second dinosaur: I give up.
First dinosaur: A drill pickle.

First dinosaur: What do you get if you cross a shark with a parrot?
Second dinosaur: Who knows?
First dinosaur: An animal that talks your ear off.

First dinosaur: Did you hear about the rabbit with the lisp who went to the dentist to get his tooth extracted?
Second dinosaur: Nope.
First dinosaur: The dentist asked him if he wanted gas, and the rabbit answered, "No, I'm an ether bunny."

First dinosaur: What is a musical fish?
Second dinosaur: My mind is a blank.
First dinosaur: A piano-tuna.

First dinosaur: What animal are you like when
you take a bath?
Second dinosaur: That's a mystery.
First dinosaur: A little bear.

First dinosaur: What animal uses a nutcracker?
Second dinosaur: I'm blank.
First dinosaur: A toothless squirrel.

First dinosaur: In what kind of home does the
buffalo roam?
Second dinosaur: I don't have the foggiest.
First dinosaur: A dirty one.

First dinosaur: What do you get if you cross a
small bear and a cow?
Second dinosaur: It's unknown to me.
First dinosaur: Winnie the Moo.

First dinosaur: What do you call a sheep that
hangs out with 40 thieves?
Second dinosaur: I'm in the dark.
First dinosaur: Ali Baa Baa.

First dinosaur: Why do birds fly south?
Second dinosaur: Search me.
First dinosaur: If they walked, it would be winter
by the time they got there.

First dinosaur: Did you hear about the silly hiker
who bought a sleeping bag?
Second dinosaur: You've got me guessing.
First dinosaur: He spent three weeks trying to
wake the bag up.

First dinosaur: What do you get if you blow your hair dryer down a rabbit hole?
Second dinosaur: I pass.
First dinosaur: Hot cross bunnies.

First dinosaur: Which skunk smells the worst?
Second dinosaur: How should I know?
First dinosaur: The one with the cheapest perfume.

Dangerous Dinosaurs

Q: How do dinosaurs earn extra money?
A: They baby-sit for bluebirds on Saturday nights!

Q: How do you know what a dinosaur is going to charge?
A: When he shows his credit card

Q: How do you get down from a dinosaur?
A: You don't. You get down from a goose.

Q: Why did the dinosaur walk around in polka-dot socks?
A: Someone stole his sneakers.

Q: How do you make a statue of a dinosaur?
A: Take a block of stone and carve away every-
    thing that doesn't look like a dinosaur.

Q: How do you get four dinosaurs in a VW bug?
A: Two in the back and two in the front.

Q: How do you make two dinosaurs float?
A: Put them on top of two scoops of ice cream in
    a big glass of soda.

Q: What's green on the inside and red and white
   on the outside?
A: Campbell's cream of dinosaur soup.

Q: Why do dinosaurs wear dark glasses?
A: If you had all those jokes told about you, you
    wouldn't want to be recognized either!

Q: What's a hitchhiking dinosaur called?
A: Stranded.

Q: What do you do when a dinosaur sits on your hanky?
A: Wait for him to get up.

Q: How do you know when there's a dinosaur in your custard?
A: When it's ever so lumpy.

Q: How do you get a rhinoceros in a VW bug?
A: Chuck one of the dinosaurs out.

Q: What would happen if a dinosaur sat in front of you in class?
A: You'd never see the blackboard.

Q: What's big and red and hides its face in the corner?
A: An embarrassed dinosaur.

Q: Why do dinosaurs wear sandals?
A: To keep their feet from sinking in the sand.

Q: What do you call a dinosaur hitchhiker?
A: A ten-and-a-half-ton pickup.

Q: How do you get a dinosaur into a matchbox?
A: Take out the matches first.

Q: Why do dinosaurs have red eyes?
A: So they can hide in cherry trees.

Dining with the Dinosaurs

Dinosaur: Waiter, why does my tea have a fly in it?
Waiter: For a cup of tea that costs 60 cents, what do you want to have fall into it—a dinosaur?

Dinosaur: Waiter, there's a fly in my stew.
Waiter: They don't care what they eat, do they?

Dinosaur: Waiter! What's this fly doing in my alphabet soup?
Waiter: Learning to read, sir!

Dinosaur: Waiter! There's a fly in my chow mein!
Waiter: That's nothing. Wait till you see what's in
   your fortune cookie.

Dinosaur: I would like a crocodile sandwich,
   please, and make it snappy!

Dinosaur: Have you any wild duck?
Waiter: No, sir, but we can take a tame one and
   irritate it for you.

Dinosaur: Waiter, there's a bee in my soup!
Waiter: Yes, sir; it's the fly's day off.

Sign outside restaurant:
DON'T STAND OUTSIDE AND BE MISERABLE.
COME INSIDE, EAT A DINOSAUR,
AND GET FED UP.

Dinosaur: Waiter, what's this fly doing in my ice cream?
Waiter: Looks like it's learning to ski.

Waiter: Sir, we are famous for snails here.
Dinosaur: I thought so. I've been served by one already.

Dinosaur: Waiter, have you ever been to the zoo?
Waiter: No, sir.
Dinosaur: Well, you ought to go. You'd enjoy seeing the turtles whizzing by.

Dinosaur: Are you the lad who took my order?
Waiter: Yes, sir.
Dinosaur: Bless me, how you've grown!

Dinosaur: Waiter, there's a piece of canvas in my fish.
Waiter: Why not? It's a sailfish.

Dinosaur: Take back this steak. I've been trying to cut it for ten minutes, but it's so tough I can't make a dent in it.

Waiter: I'm sorry, sir, but I can't take it back. You've bent it.

More Delightful Dinosaurs

First dinosaur: Why shouldn't you cry when a cow falls on the ice?
Second dinosaur: Beats me.
First dinosaur: Because it's no use crying over spilled milk.

First dinosaur: What is the name of your dog?
Second dinosaur: Ginger.
First dinosaur: Does Ginger bite?
Second dinosaur: No, Ginger snaps!

First dinosaur: Why can't you talk with a goat around?
Second dinosaur: I can't guess.
First dinosaur: He's always butting in.

First dinosaur: The woolly mammoth was
    arrested for stealing a pig.
Second dinosaur: How did they prove it?
First dinosaur: The pig squealed.

First dinosaur: What do you call a donkey who
    carries a man?
Second dinosaur: I have no idea.
First dinosaur: A he-hauler.

First dinosaur: What's black and white and red
    all over?
Second dinosaur: You tell me.
First dinosaur: A sunburned zebra.

First dinosaur: What's white outside, green
    inside, and hops?
Second dinosaur: I give up.
First dinosaur: A frog sandwich.

First dinosaur: Name six things smaller than an ant's mouth.
Second dinosaur: I can't.
First dinosaur: Six of his teeth.

First dinosaur: What did the mountain climber yell when he saw the avalanche?
Second dinosaur: Who knows?
First dinosaur: Here come the Rolling Stones!

First dinosaur: Why was the insect kicked out of the national park?
Second dinosaur: You've got me.
First dinosaur: Because it was a litterbug.

First dinosaur: How does a nut feel when a squirrel chews on it?
Second dinosaur: My mind is a blank.
First dinosaur: Nut so good.

First dinosaur: What do you get if you cross a skunk and a boomerang?

Second dinosaur: That's a mystery.
First dinosaur: A smell you can't get rid of.

First dinosaur: If my cat won an Oscar, what would he get?
Second dinosaur: I'm blank.
First dinosaur: The a-cat-emy award.

First dinosaur: What animal doesn't play fair?
Second dinosaur: I don't have the foggiest.
First dinosaur: A cheetah.

First dinosaur: How does an octopus go into battle?
Second dinosaur: It's unknown to me.
First dinosaur: Well armed.

First dinosaur: Why did the city rat gnaw a hole in the carpet?
Second dinosaur: Search me.
First dinosaur: He wanted to see the floor show.

First dinosaur: Did you hear about the horse who ate an electric wire instead of hay?
Second dinosaur: You've got me guessing.
First dinosaur: He went haywire.

First dinosaur: What's black and white and red all over?
Second dinosaur: I pass.
First dinosaur: A sunburned penguin.

First dinosaur: What kind of story is the story about the three little pigs?
Second dinosaur: How should I know?
First dinosaur: A pigtail.

24

Dainty Dinosaurs

Q: How do dinosaurs dive into swimming pools?
A: Head first.

Q: If you shoot a white dinosaur with a white
   gun, what do you shoot a pink dinosaur with?
A: You paint the dinosaur white, then shoot it
   with a white gun.

Q: Why can't dinosaurs fly?
A: They don't have propellers.

First woolly mammoth: Why did the dinosaurs
   paint their toenails red?
Second woolly mammoth: I don't know. Why?

First woolly mammoth: So they could hide in the strawberry patch. Did you ever see a dinosaur in a strawberry patch?
Second woolly mammoth: No!
First woolly mammoth: That proves it works.

First woolly mammoth: Is a dinosaur big enough to eat when it's two weeks old?
Second woolly mammoth: Of course not.
First woolly mammoth: Well, then how does it manage to live?

Q: Why did the dinosaur paint her head yellow?
A: She wanted to see if blondes had more fun.

Q: Why do dinosaurs have wrinkles?
A: Have you ever tried to iron one?

Q: How do you get a dinosaur out of a Jell-O box?
A: Read the directions on the back.

Q: How do you know when there's a dinosaur in the refrigerator?
A: You can see his footprints in the cheesecake.

Q: What is the difference between a dinosaur and a flea?
A: A dinosaur can have a flea, but a flea can't have a dinosaur.

Q: What is green and hangs on a tree?
A: An unripened dinosaur.

Q: What did the psychiatrist say to the dinosaur?
A: That'll be $30 for the visit…and $300 for the couch.

Q: Does your dinosaur bite strangers?
A: Only when he doesn't know them.

Q: Why did the dinosaur swim on his back?
A: So he wouldn't get his tennis shoes wet.

Recipe for dinosaur stew:

One dinosaur, two rabbits (optional), salt, and pepper. Cut the dinosaur into small bite-size pieces. This should take about two months. Add enough brown gravy to cover. Cook over kerosene stove for about four weeks at 464 degrees. This will serve 3800 people. If more are expected, two rabbits may be added, but do this only if necessary because most people do not like to find hares in their stew.

Woolly Mammoths' Knock, Knock Jokes

First woolly mammoth: Knock, knock.
Second woolly mammoth: Who's there?
First woolly mammoth: Franz.
Second woolly mammoth: Franz who?
First woolly mammoth: Franz, Romans,
    Countrymen, lend me your ears.

First woolly mammoth: Knock, knock.
Second woolly mammoth: Who's there?
First woolly mammoth: Diane.
Second woolly mammoth: Diane who?
First woolly mammoth: Diane to meet you!

First woolly mammoth: Knock, knock.
Second woolly mammoth: Who's there?
First woolly mammoth: Orange.
Second woolly mammoth: Orange who?
First woolly mammoth: Orange you even going
to open the door?

First woolly mammoth: Knock, knock.
Second woolly mammoth: Who's there?
First woolly mammoth: Cash.
Second woolly mammoth: Cash who?
First woolly mammoth: Cash me if you can!

First woolly mammoth: Knock, knock.
Second woolly mammoth: Who's there?
First woolly mammoth: Gus.
Second woolly mammoth: Gus who?
First woolly mammoth: Gus you don't want to
play.

First woolly mammoth: Knock, knock.
Second woolly mammoth: Who's there?
First woolly mammoth: Hank.

Second woolly mammoth: Hank who?
First woolly mammoth: Hank you for opening
the door.

First woolly mammoth: Knock, knock.
Second woolly mammoth: Who's there?
First woolly mammoth: Sherwood.
Second woolly mammoth: Sherwood who?
First woolly mammoth: Sherwood be nice to have
you open the door.

First woolly mammoth: Knock, knock.
Second woolly mammoth: Who's there?
First woolly mammoth: Esau.
Second woolly mammoth: Esau who?
First woolly mammoth: Esau you lookin' out the
window.

First woolly mammoth: Knock, knock.
Second woolly mammoth: Who's there?
First woolly mammoth: Yuri.
Second woolly mammoth: Yuri who?
First woolly mammoth: Yuri great person.

First woolly mammoth: Knock, knock.
Second woolly mammoth: Who's there?
First woolly mammoth: Juan.
Second woolly mammoth: Juan who?
First woolly mammoth: Juan to hear some more knock, knock jokes?

First woolly mammoth: Knock, knock.
Second woolly mammoth: Who's there?
First woolly mammoth: Louis.
Second woolly mammoth: Louis who?
First woolly mammoth: Louis'n up—don't be so uptight!

First woolly mammoth: Knock, knock.
Second woolly mammoth: Who's there.
First woolly mammoth: Cook.
Second woolly mammoth: Cook who?
First woolly mammoth: Cut the bird impressions, I want to come in!

First woolly mammoth: Knock, knock.
Second woolly mammoth: Who's there?
First woolly mammoth: Ezra.
Second woolly mammoth: Ezra who?
First woolly mammoth: Ezra doctor in the house?

First woolly mammoth: Knock, knock.
Second woolly mammoth: Who's there?
First woolly mammoth: William.
Second woolly mammoth: William who?
First woolly mammoth: Williamind your own
    business!

First woolly mammoth: Knock, knock.
Second woolly mammoth: Who's there?
First woolly mammoth: Yoda.
Second woolly mammoth: Yoda who?
First woolly mammoth: Yodalay-hee-who!

First woolly mammoth: Knock, knock.
Second woolly mammoth: Who's there?
First woolly mammoth: Mikey.
Second woolly mammoth: Mikey who?
First woolly mammoth: Mikey won't fit in this
    lock!

First woolly mammoth: Knock, knock.
Second woolly mammoth: Who's there?
First woolly mammoth: Odessa.
Second woolly mammoth: Odessa who?
First woolly mammoth: Odessa good knock, knock joke!

First woolly mammoth: Knock, knock.
Second woolly mammoth: Who's there?
First woolly mammoth: Atlas.
Second woolly mammoth: Atlas who?
First woolly mammoth: Atlas you answered the door!

First woolly mammoth: Knock, knock.
Second woolly mammoth: Who's there?
First woolly mammoth: Noah.
Second woolly mammoth: Noah who?
First woolly mammoth: Noah one you know.

First woolly mammoth: Knock, knock.
Second woolly mammoth: Who's there?

First woolly mammoth: Isabella.
Second woolly mammoth: Isabella who?
First woolly mammoth: Isabella don't work;
that's why I am knocking.

First woolly mammoth: Knock, knock.
Second woolly mammoth: Who's there?
First woolly mammoth: Cain.
Second woolly mammoth: Cain who?
First woolly mammoth: Cain you come out to
play?

First woolly mammoth: Knock, knock.
Second woolly mammoth: Who's there?
First woolly mammoth: Colleen.
Second woolly mammoth: Colleen who?
First woolly mammoth: Colleen up your room;
it's a mess.

First woolly mammoth: Knock, knock.
Second woolly mammoth: Who's there?
First woolly mammoth: Neal.
Second woolly mammoth: Neal who?
First woolly mammoth: Neal and pray!

First woolly mammoth: Knock, knock.
Second woolly mammoth: Who's there?
First woolly mammoth: Ford.
Second woolly mammoth: Ford who?
First woolly mammoth: Ford he's a jolly good
    fellow.

First woolly mammoth: Knock, knock.
Second woolly mammoth: Who's there?
First woolly mammoth: Stalin.
Second woolly mammoth: Stalin who?
First woolly mammoth: Stalin for time!

First woolly mammoth: Knock, knock.
Second woolly mammoth: Who's there?
First woolly mammoth: Handel.
Second woolly mammoth: Handel who?
First woolly mammoth: Handel with care!

More Dinosaur Mania

First dinosaur: What does Santa use for bandages?
Second dinosaur: Santa Gauze.

First dinosaur: What can you eat on a starvation diet?
Second dinosaur: Fast food.

First dinosaur: What's the best cheese to eat when you are up a tree?
Second dinosaur: Limb-burger cheese.

First dinosaur: Why was the dolphin so sad?
Second dinosaur: It had no porpoise in life.

First dinosaur: What do you call the author of a
    Western story?
Second dinosaur: A horseback writer.

First dinosaur: How do you make friends with a
    computer?
Second dinosaur: Bit by bit.

First dinosaur: What do you call 13 sleeping
    pastry chefs?
Second dinosaur: Bakers dozin'.

First dinosaur: How does a fish pay his bills?
Second dinosaur: With a credit cod.

First dinosaur: What do computer experts eat for
    a snack?
Second dinosaur: Memory chips.

First dinosaur: What do you call a sheet
salesman?
Second dinosaur: An undercover agent.

First dinosaur: Why do some drivers have good
safety records?
Second dinosaur: Because they are wreck-less.

First dinosaur: What do you call someone who
bites a police officer?
Second dinosaur: A law a-biting citizen.

First dinosaur: What do you call a bug that hates
Christmas?
Second dinosaur: A humbug!

First dinosaur: What was the cause of Adam's
first real argument with Eve?
Second dinosaur: He caught her putting his best
Sunday suit into the salad.

First dinosaur: What do they call an ice-cream vendor in Arizona?
Second dinosaur: A good Yuma man.

First dinosaur: Did you hear the joke about the moon?
Second dinosaur: Yeah, it's far out!

First dinosaur: If you were walking alongside a donkey, what fruit would you represent?
Second dinosaur: A pear.

First dinosaur: Where do salmon go to sleep?
Second dinosaur: On the river bed.

First dinosaur: How many monkeys can you put into an empty barrel?
Second dinosaur: One. After that the barrel isn't empty.

First dinosaur: How do sailors get their clothes clean?
Second dinosaur: They throw them overboard, and then they are washed ashore.

First dinosaur: What is green, noisy, and extremely dangerous?
Second dinosaur: A stampeding herd of pickles.

First dinosaur: Why do birds hang around libraries?
Second dinosaur: To catch bookworms.

First dinosaur: What do you feed a hungry cheer-leading squad?
Second dinosaur: Cheer-ios!

27

Harry Gorilla

Q: What did they make Harry Gorilla do when he drew a line three blocks long at his movie?
A: They made him erase it!

Q: What do you have when you give Harry Gorilla a piggyback ride?
A: A monkey on your back.

Q: What would you get if you crossed Harry Gorilla with a roach?
A: We don't know—but you'd better not step on him!

Q: Why did Harry Gorilla keep falling out of the tree?
A: Because he built his tree house upside down!

Q: If you were Harry Gorilla's brother and he had a baby boy, what would that make you?
A: A monkey's uncle!

Q: Why did Harry Gorilla go on a diet?
A: So he could fit into his Volkswagen!

Q: Why did Harry Gorilla take a sleeping pill with a reducing pill?
A: Because he wanted to take a light nap!

Q: Why does Harry Gorilla want to get rid of his red china?
A: Because it clashes with his purple tablecloth!

Q: When do you give Harry Gorilla a going-away present?
A: When you want him to go away!

Q: What happened when Harry Gorilla took a midnight stroll through New York City?
A: He got mugged.

Q: What do you call the woman who marries Harry Gorilla?
A: Mrs. Gorilla.

Q: Why should you never hit Harry Gorilla when he's down?
A: He might get up!

Q: How do you stop Harry Gorilla from burping?
A: Hold him over your shoulder!

Q: How do you shake hands with Harry Gorilla?
A: Very carefully!

More Daffy Dinosaurs

Q: Why do dinosaurs wear shorts?
A: You'd sweat too if you wore long pants in the jungle heat!

Q: How do you catch a dinosaur?
A: First you take a pair of tweezers, binoculars, a milk carton, and a sign that has "dinosaur" spelled wrong. Then you take the sign into a jungle, hang it from a tree, and wait for a dinosaur to come along and correct the spelling. While he's figuring out how to do it, you look at him through the wrong end of the binoculars, pick him up with the tweezers, and put him in the milk carton.

Q: What's the difference between a dinosaur and peanut butter?
A: A dinosaur won't stick to the roof of your mouth.

Q: How do you get a dinosaur into a telephone booth?
A: Open the door.

Q: Why can't a dinosaur ride a bicycle?
A: Because he has no thumbs to ring the bell.

Q: What did the dinosaur say to the platypus?
A: I never forget a face, but with yours I'll make an exception.

Q: What can you say about nine dinosaurs wearing pink sneakers and one dinosaur wearing blue?
A: Nine out of ten dinosaurs wear pink sneakers.

Q: Why did the dinosaur paint himself all different colors?
A: So he could hide in a package of M&M's.

Q: How do you stop a dinosaur passing through the eye of a needle?
A: Tie a knot in its tail.

Q: What do you do with old bowling balls?
A: Give them to the dinosaurs to shoot marbles with.

Q: What did the grape say when the dinosaur stepped on it?
A: Nothing—it just let out a little whine.

Q: How do you get a dinosaur into a popcorn box?
A: You don't. They only come in Crackerjacks.

More Dizzy Dinosaurs

First dinosaur: Did you hear about the cross-eyed teacher?
Second dinosaur: No, I didn't.
First dinosaur: He had no control over his pupils.

First dinosaur: I'm going to have to write a letter to your parents about this poor essay.
Second dinosaur: I wouldn't do that.
First dinosaur: Why not?
Second dinosaur: They wrote it.

First dinosaur: Do fish perspire?
Second dinosaur: Naturally. What do you think makes the sea salty?

First dinosaur: I'm studying to be a barber.
Second dinosaur: Will it take long?
First dinosaur: No, I'm learning all the short cuts.

First dinosaur: I've changed my mind.
Second dinosaur: Thank goodness! Does it work
    better now?

First dinosaur: Don't you like music?
Second dinosaur: I certainly do. I have a zither at
    home.
First dinosaur: Really? I have a brother at home.
Second dinosaur: No, you don't understand. A
    zither is a sort of lyre.
First dinosaur: Yeah, my brother is a liar, too.

First dinosaur: What did your teacher say when
    you told her you were an only child?
Second dinosaur: She said, "Thank goodness!"

First dinosaur: When I grow up, I want to be a
vitamin.
Second dinosaur: Don't be silly. You can't be a
vitamin.
First dinosaur: Yes, I can. I saw a sign in a store
window that said "Vitamin B-1."

First dinosaur: What was one benefit of the
invention of the automobile?
Second dinosaur: It reduced horse-stealing.

First dinosaur: Excuse me for living!
Second dinosaur: All right, but don't let it
happen again.

First dinosaur: Where is Moscow located?
Second dinosaur: In the barn with Pa's cow.

First dinosaur: I'll have you know that everyone
in my block looks to me for advice and fol-
lows it!
Second dinosaur: I don't doubt it. You're a natural–born blockhead.

First dinosaur: Am I crazy if I talk to myself?
Second dinosaur: No, but you are if you pay any
    attention.

First dinosaur: Define natural death.
Second dinosaur: Dying without a doctor's help.

First dinosaur: Today I received an anonymous
    letter.
Second dinosaur: Oh, from whom?

First dinosaur: I'm so worried. I keep thinking
    I'm a pair of drapes.
Second dinosaur: Don't worry. Pull yourself
    together!

My dinosaur used to think he was a canary. But
    he went to a marvelous psychiatrist, and now
    we don't hear a peep out of him.

30

Dribbling Dinosaurs

Q: Why does a dinosaur have cracks between his toes?
A: To carry his library card.

Fred: What's the difference between a lemon, a dinosaur, and a tube of glue?
Barney: I give up.
Fred: You can squeeze a lemon, but you can't squeeze a dinosaur.
Barney: What about the tube of glue?
Fred: That's where you get stuck.

Q: Why don't more dinosaurs join the police force?
A: They can't hide behind the billboards.

Q: Why did the dinosaur walk on two legs?
A: To give the ants a chance.

Q: Why is it dangerous to go into the jungle
  between two and four in the afternoon?
A: Because that's when dinosaurs are jumping
  out of palm trees!

Q: Why do dinosaurs have long toenails on
  Friday?
A: Because their pedicurist doesn't come until
  Saturday!

Q: What did Fred Flintstone say when he saw the
  dinosaurs coming down the path wearing
  sunglasses?
A: Nothing! He couldn't recognize them!

Q: Why don't dinosaurs take ballet lessons?
A: a. They outgrew their leotards!
   b. They learned how to dance in the circus!
   c. They'd rather learn how to play Monopoly!

Q: Why do dinosaurs have wrinkles in their knees?
A: a. From old age!
   b. From playing marbles!
   c. Because they worry too much!

Q: Why do dinosaurs climb trees?
A: a. To get in their nests!
   b. There's nothing else to climb in the jungle!
   c. Because they think it's lots of fun to do.

Q: Why did I buy this ridiculous dinosaur joke book?
A: a. Because I had $4.99 to waste!
   b. Because I didn't know better!
   c. Because I'm sick!

Q: Why did the dinosaur fall out of a palm tree?
A: A hippopotamus pushed him out!

Q: Why do dinosaurs have flat feet?
A: They don't have arches in their sneakers!

Q: How can you tell if a dinosaur is visiting your house?
A: His tricycle will be parked outside.

Q: Why did the dinosaur lie on his back in the water and stick his feet up?
A: So you could tell him from a bar of Ivory soap!

Q: Why do dinosaurs wear glasses?
A: To make sure they don't step on other dinosaurs!

Q: What do you know when you see three
dinosaurs walking down the street wearing
pink sweatshirts?

A: a. They belong to your school chess club.
b. They're all on the same basketball team.
c. You need a psychiatrist. (Who ever heard of
three dinosaurs walking down the street
wearing pink sweatshirts?)

Q: What's red on the outside and green on the
inside?

A: a. A dinosaur wearing red pajamas!
b. A dinosaur swimming in the Red Sea!
c. Campbell's cream of dinosaur soup!

Other Books by Bob Phillips